New Dimensions
IN THE
WORLD OF READING

Morning Bells

P R O G R A M   A U T H O R S

James F. Baumann   Roselmina Indrisano   P. David Pearson
Theodore Clymer   Dale D. Johnson   Taffy E. Raphael
Carl Grant   Connie Juel   Marian Davies Toth
Elfrieda H. Hiebert   Jeanne R. Paratore   Richard L. Venezky

Contributing Author: Rosann Englebretson

COVER ILLUSTRATOR
Spotlight

Robin Spowart

● Robin Spowart loves to paint pictures for children's books. He also talks to children about how he paints.

● He likes to make changes in his pictures, so he uses paint he can change. The rabbit on the back cover once had a yellow dress. The artist says, "I changed my mind and made it pink!"

SILVER BURDETT GINN

NEEDHAM, MA   MORRISTOWN, NJ

ATLANTA, GA   DALLAS, TX   DEERFIELD, IL   MENLO PARK, CA

Theme

All About Us

All About Us

No two families are the same!

✳ Read *Moja Means One* by Muriel Feelings to learn about the games children play in East Africa.

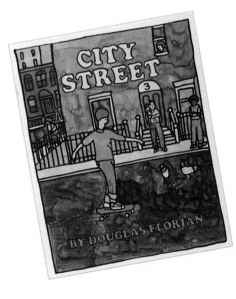

✳ See what keeps a neighborhood busy and full of fun in *City Street* by Douglas Florian.

Barksbee BOOKS

❊ Read about holidays in *Our Family Celebrates* by Lindsay Rollins.

❊ Hold on tight for *Roller Coaster Ride* by Zachary Judd.

❊ Bobby's little brother Petey can be a monster! Find out if the brothers will ever get along in *Petey* by Deborah Eaton.

❊ Where is Josephine? Help with the search in *Josephine Takes a Spin* by D. Marion.

Brother John

Are you sleeping?
Are you sleeping?

Brother John,
Brother John,

Morning bells are ringing!
Morning bells are ringing!

DING, DONG, DING!
DING, DONG, DING!

SING ALONG

Twins, Twins, Twins

Written by Zachary Judd

Some twins are brothers.

Some are sisters.

Some are brothers *and* sisters.

Some twins look just alike.

Some look different.

Twins have the same family.
They have the same birthday.

Some twins are cute babies.
Some are kids just like you.

Some twins are grownups, too.

Would you like to be a twin?
Think about what it would be like.

Growing Up

When I was seven
We went for a picnic
Up to a magic
Foresty place.
I knew there were tigers
Behind every boulder,
Though I didn't meet one
Face to face.

When I was older
We went for a picnic
Up to the very same
Place as before,
And all of the trees
And the rocks were so little
They couldn't hide tigers
Or *me* anymore.

Harry Behn

Marvin's Moon Flight

written by Winston White • illustrated by Catherine O'Neill

"Let's go to the moon," said Marvin to his mother.
"I'm building a rocket in the yard."

"I'm too busy, Marvin," said his mother.
"I have to wash the car. You go and have a good time."

21

"Want to go to the moon with me?" Marvin asked his sister, Anita. "I'm building a rocket in the yard."

"I'm too busy," said Anita. "I have to go to soccer practice. You go and have a good time."

"How would you like to go to
the moon?" Marvin asked his brother,
Wilson. "I'm building a rocket in
the yard."

"I'm too busy," said Wilson. "I have
to study for my spelling test. You go
and have a good time."

"Will you come to the moon with me?" Marvin asked his other brother, Thomas. "I'm building a rocket in the yard."

"I'm too busy," said Thomas. "I have to fix my computer. You go and have a good time."

24

Since none of his family would go with him,
Marvin went to the moon all by himself.

25

He had a **very** good time.
And he even brought back
moon rocks for the whole family.

Next time Mother and Anita and Wilson and
Thomas want to go to the moon with Marvin.

But Marvin is already building
an underwater diving machine
in the yard.

32

SHOES FROM GRANDPA

by MEM FOX • Illustrated by PATRICIA MULLINS

LATE one summer Jessie's father
invited all the family over for a barbecue.

When Grandpa saw Jessie he stood back and said,
"My, how you've grown! You'll need a new pair
of shoes this winter, and I'll buy them."

37

38

"Thanks a lot, Grandpa," said Jessie.

Then her dad said,
"I'll buy you some socks from the local shops,
to go with the shoes from Grandpa."

41

And her mom said,
"I'll buy you a skirt that won't show the dirt,
to go with the socks from the local shops,
to go with the shoes from Grandpa."

And her cousin said,
"I'll look for a blouse with ribbons and bows,
to go with the skirt that won't show the dirt,
to go with the socks from the local shops,
to go with the shoes from Grandpa."

And her sister said,
"I'll get you a sweater when the weather gets wetter,
to go with the blouse with ribbons and bows,
to go with the skirt that won't show the dirt,
to go with the socks from the local shops,
to go with the shoes from Grandpa."

And her grandma said,
"I'll find you a coat you could wear on a boat,
to go with the sweater when the weather gets wetter,
to go with the blouse with ribbons and bows,
to go with the skirt that won't show the dirt,
to go with the socks from the local shops,
to go with the shoes from Grandpa."

48

And her aunt said,
"I'll knit you a scarf that'll make us all laugh,
to go with the coat you could wear on a boat,
to go with the sweater when the weather gets wetter,
to go with the blouse with ribbons and bows,

to go with the skirt that won't show the dirt,
to go with the socks from the local shops,
to go with the shoes from Grandpa.''

And her brother said,
"I'll find you a hat you can put on like that,
to go with the scarf that'll make us all laugh,
to go with the coat you could wear on a boat,
to go with the sweater when the weather gets wetter,
to go with the blouse with ribbons and bows,
to go with the skirt that won't show the dirt,
to go with the socks from the local shops,
to go with the shoes from Grandpa."

54

And her uncle said,
"I'll buy you some mittens that are softer than kittens,
to go with the hat you can put on like that,
to go with the scarf that'll make us all laugh,
to go with the coat you could wear on a boat,

SOCKS

HATS

to go with the sweater when the weather gets wetter,
to go with the blouse with ribbons and bows,
to go with the skirt that won't show the dirt,
to go with the socks from the local shops,
to go with the shoes from Grandpa.''

And Jessie said,
"You're all so kind that I hate to be mean,
but please, would one of you buy me some jeans?"

61

The Wrong Start

I got up this morning and meant to be good,
But things didn't happen the way that they should.

    I lost my toothbrush,
        I slammed the door,
    I dropped an egg
        On the kitchen floor,
    I spilled some sugar
        And after that
    I tried to hurry
        And tripped on the cat.

Things may get better. I don't know when.
I think I'll go back and start over again.

                            Marchette Chute

One of Three

ANGELA JOHNSON
pictures by DAVID SOMAN

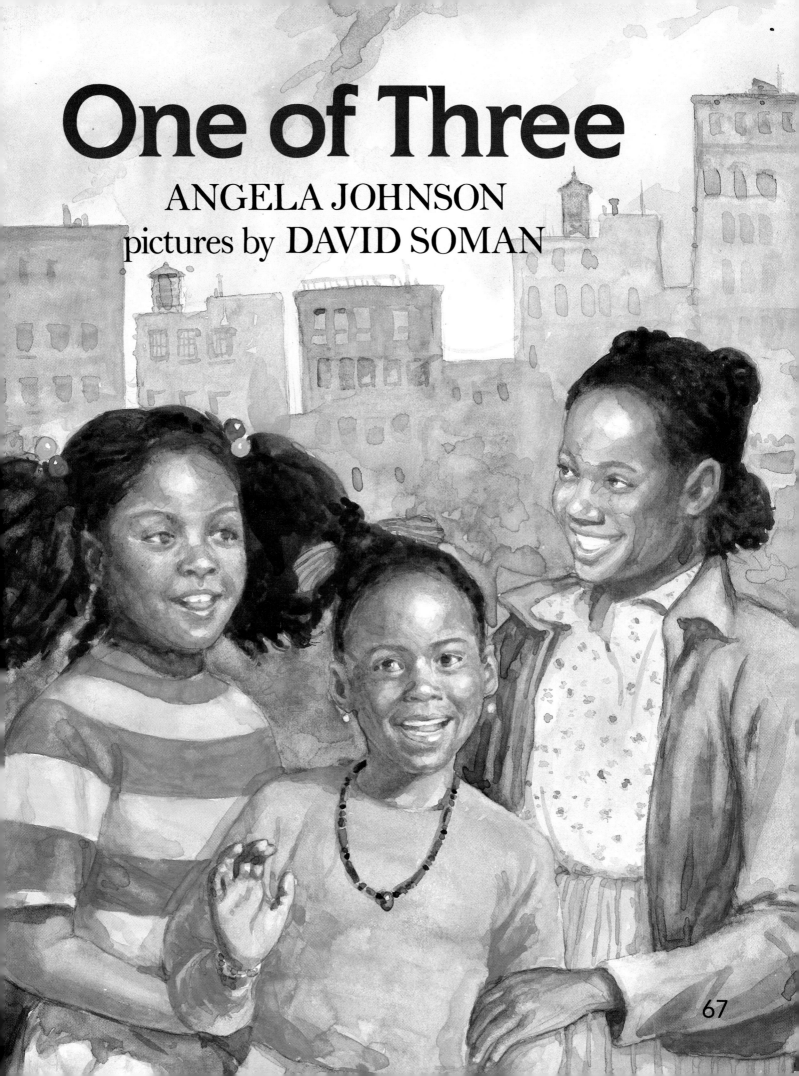

Since I can remember I've been one of three.
Eva, Nikki, and me.

One of three sisters that walk to school together.
Down the street together.
One of the three in the sun and the rain.

I'm one of the three that lives in apartment number 2,
has long hair and brown eyes, and can sometimes
play hopscotch by the trash cans
if I ask for a long time.

On Saturdays I'm one of the three that sits
outside the bakery and looks and smells and smells....

I'm one of the three that squeezes into the taxi
on snowy days with Mama, Aunt Sara, and Grandma,
and it's warm there.

76

I'm one of the three that looks just like our mama,
smiles just like our daddy,
and holds hands with my sisters in the store,
looking like triplets—almost.

I'm one of the three that likes the subway,
the people on it,
and the way our feet hang over the seats.

I'm one of three who lives over the flower shop.
Mr. Lowen still gets all of our names wrong,
but he gives us each a daisy every time.

83

We walk down the street like stairsteps,
and I'm in front.

Sometimes Eva and Nikki say
I'm not invited to go with them.
Not to the park, the store,
or sometimes even for a walk.

I'm left behind.
Not one of three, just one.

Then Mama calls me Sister and says I'm too little
to go there or do that,
so maybe I just want to help her paint or read to her.

Daddy says that I have to be the baby sometimes,
and keep Mama and him company,
just sometimes.

I miss Eva and Nikki and me....
But when it's just Mama, Daddy, and me,
it's a different kind of three,
and that's fine too....

96

Chicka Chicka Boom Boom

by Bill Martin Jr
and John Archambault

A told B
and B told C,
I'll meet you at the top
of the coconut tree.

98

READ ALOUD

Whee! said D
and E F G.
We'll beat you to the top
of the coconut tree.

READ ALOUD

Chicka chicka boom boom!
Will there be enough room?
Here comes H
up the coconut tree.

And I and J and tag-along K,
all on their way
up the coconut tree.

READ ALOUD

Chicka chicka boom boom!
Will there be enough room?
Can you believe it?
Here's L M N O P!

And Q R S!

104

And T U V!

105

And still more! W!
and X Y Z!

READ ALOUD

The whole alphabet
up the—Oh no . . .

Chicka chicka

BOOM! BOOM!

READ ALOUD

ABOUT THE
Authors & Illustrators

Mem Fox

Mem Fox lives in Australia. She has two jobs. She teaches people who want to be teachers and she has another job. She also likes to write books for children. *Shoes from Grandpa* is one of her books. You might have read *Hattie and the Fox*. She wrote that one, too.

Angela Johnson

Angela Johnson grew up in a family
of storytellers. Every night her father
and grandfather would tell stories to
the family. Angela Johnson thought
she would like to write stories for
children. She writes good stories
about growing up in her family.
One of Three is one of those stories.

Bill Martin Jr

Bill Martin grew up in the state of Kansas. When he was growing up, he loved to listen to his grandmother tell family stories. Before he became a writer, he was a teacher and a storyteller. Bill Martin has written many stories for children. Look for them in the library.

John Archambault

John Archambault writes poems and stories. He's a storyteller, too. He has written many books with Bill Martin Jr. Many of them have won awards. Some of their books, like *The Ghost-Eye Tree, Barn Dance!,* and *Knots on a Counting Rope,* have been on *Reading Rainbow.*